SECOND EDITION.

By Order of the Trustees of the Will of the late Mr. WILLIAM CROSS.

TO BREWERS, PUBLICANS & OTHERS.

∾ ESSEX. ∾

Particulars Plan and Conditions of Sale of the

FULLY LICENSED

FREEHOLD AND COPYHOLD

Hotels and Public Houses,

BEER HOUSE, AND ALSO BUILDING AND ACCOMMODATION LAND,

COMPRISING

"The Castle Hotel," Southend=on=Sea.

"The Griffin Hotel," Danbury.

"The Golden Lion Hotel,"

AND

"The Paul Pry Beer House," Rayleigh.

"The Bell Inn," Great Wakering.

"The Lobster Smack," Canvey Island.

"The Windmill Inn," East Hanningfield,

AND

PASTURE LAND ADJOINING.

"The Green Man Inn," Bradwell=on=Sea,

AND

BUILDING LAND ADJOINING.

"The Rose & Crown Inn," Southminster,

AND

BUILDING LAND ADJOINING.

WITH POSSESSION OF THE WHOLE AT MICHAELMAS, 1905.

MESSRS. TUCKETT & SON

are instructed to Sell by Auction

At the **MART**, Tokenhouse Yard, London, E.C.,

On Monday, 3rd July, 1905, at 2 o'clock precisely,

the above valuable Properties in 12 LOTS.

Particulars with Plan and Conditions of Sale may be obtained of
MESSRS. WOOD, SON & LANGTON, SOLICITORS, CLARENCE STREET, SOUTHEND-ON-SEA;
at the Mart, of the several Hotels and Inns forming this Sale; and of

Messrs. TUCKETT & SON, Auctioneers, Surveyors, & Land Agents,

The east view of the Holy Trinity Church in 1830. To the left is the old school room which was later demolished and replaced by a new school. This became the National School for boys, and then the parish room.

RAYLEIGH
A Pictorial History

Ernest H. Lane &
Edward FitzGerald

Phillimore

1991

Published by
PHILLIMORE & CO. LTD.
Shopwyke Hall, Chichester, Sussex

ISBN 0 85033 810 7

Printed and bound in Great Britain by
BIDDLES LTD.
Guildford, Surrey

This book is dedicated to the many helpers engaged
in the Fairhaven Hospice
which serves the community in south-east Essex
to whom any profits from the sale of this book will be donated.

List of Illustrations

Frontispiece: Holy Trinity Church

Acknowledgements

The decision to publish this pictorial history came in response to the growing concern that those who knew the village before its sudden population growth were getting fewer and fewer in number, and that their valuable collections were either scattered or destroyed.

We are indebted to the many who willingly offered pictures and other information and, from well over 400 such contributions, have selected what we feel reflects the general desire to place on record the most interesting aspects of Rayleigh's past.

We wish to record our special thanks to Mr. M. J. Ball ARPS for the diligent manner in which he so willingly reproduced many of the pictures and slides. Without his sterling services it is doubtful whether we could have produced this book.

Thanks are also recorded to Mr. R. Byford, Mrs. S. D. Green, trustee of Rayleigh Mill Museum, Mr. Peter Lewis, Mr. J. D. Nash, Mrs. E. Kemp, Miss M. Gale, Mr. D. D. Ager and Mr. K. Gee, Chairman of the Civic Society.

For their patience and interest in typing the introduction and the numerous captions, itself a very daunting task, we were fortunate to have the help of Mrs. Pullinger (courtesy of Mr. G. Hawkes, Manager of Barclays Bank, Rayleigh), Mrs. B. Emery (through the good offices of A. T. Richards of Rona Partnership) and Mrs. J. Lantaff.

We were encouraged by Mr. May, Manager of Rayleigh Library and his staff; the officers of Southend Museum Services and Evening Echo newspapers, who granted us access to their files.

Finally, a big thank-you to the following who contributed pictures, whether published or not. This response made the creation of the first pictorial history of Rayleigh possible:
D. Ager, Miss. G. Alderton, E. Baker, M. Ball, D. Barber, K. Bocking, Mrs. J. Boyes, D. and M. Burton, R. Carpenter, Mrs. E. Clover, R. Cottis, J. Cotton, Mrs. E. Crouch, Mrs. V. Cubbit, D. Dowling, Rev. P. Elliott, R. Fletcher, Mrs. I. Franklin, A. Gabbitas, Miss. M. Gale, W. Gale, Mrs. M. Galley, S. Goodwin, E. Harris, Mrs. J. Harrison, J. Jackson, Mrs. P. Jones, Mrs. T. Keys, Mrs. E. Kemp, H. C. Lane, P. Lewis, Mrs. F. Matthews, R. McEwen, H. Nash, Mrs. M. Norton, Mrs. B. Phillips, R. Pilgrim, M. Reedman, Rayleigh Museum Collection, H. Revering, Mrs. M. Shirley, M. Shorter, Mrs. J. Storey, E. Stratford, Mrs. K. Stringer, R. Todman, B. Tregenza, United Reformed church, Mrs. E. Woolhouse and J. Stock of the Salvation Army.

Copyright Southend Museum Services: 31, 54, 95, 123, 135, 136, 157, 163, 171; Evening Echo: 107, 147; County Guide Publications, 2.

Introduction

Rayleigh has been a place of habitation since before 6000 B.C. Primitive paleolithic, mesolithic and neolithic tribes have left traces of their settlement, such as flints, tools and weapons, at nearby Hamborough (Hambro) Hill and Hullbridge. The site, some 240 ft. above sea level, was not only secure but close to the coast, so that settlers were able to fish as well as hunt for their food.

The Bronze Age brought the Kimmerians and, a little later, the Beaker-folk to the area. These were followed by the *Trinovantes*. When Caesar invaded Britain in 55/54 B.C., this powerful tribe attempted to seek protection from the warlike Belgic tribes who were raiding from the south. Roman settlement was extensive, and their red tiles may be seen in the fabric of Holy Trinity church, Rayleigh. A hoard of coins has also been found nearby at White House Farm, in Eastwood Road. Unearthed in 1850, over 200 were discovered in an earthenware pot.

After four centuries of occupation the Romans withdrew from Britain, in 420. The Picts and Scots invaded, and the Dark Ages began – 'dark' through lack of historical evidence.

Until the arrival of the East Saxons *c.*527 there is little further evidence of settlement in the Rayleigh area. Although they divided their territory into 'hundreds' for the purpose of government, little evidence remains of the East Saxons' stay. However they named the county and Rayleigh itself. Raege (a wild she-goat, or doe), and leah (a clearing). Before the 14th century there were over 50 ways of spelling the name, for example, Raghleia, Raleigh and Rayleg.

On the eve of the Norman Conquest in 1066, Rayleigh was entering its most important period. The estate was owned by Robert FitzWimarc, who was Sheriff of Essex, Constable and King's Standard Bearer. His success continued under King William, who rewarded Robert's support before the Battle of Hastings with many favours. The only pre-Norman landowner in the whole of Essex to retain his titles and lands, Robert passed his estates to Swein his son who, by 1086, when the Domesday Survey was undertaken, was lord of 67 estates in the county. Swein's importance was such that he was buried in Westminster Abbey. His son, another Robert, built Prittlewell Priory, which was a small community of Cluniac monks, but the FitzWimarc line was disgraced in the next generation. Henry de Essex, Robert's son, became Constable of England, but disgraced himself in a battle at Coleshall in Wales (?1163), when he cried 'the king is dead', threw down the standard, and fled. Charged with cowardice, he forfeited the barony to the Crown.

Hubert de Burgh, Justiciar of England and later Earl of Kent, was next to be granted the barony, and *c.*1225 he began to hold a market there. The market finally fell into disuse *c.*1818. By 1249 the estate had passed to the Countess of Kent, who sued her neighbour the Earl of Oxford in that year, for setting up market at Prittlewell to the injury of her market in Rayleigh. At this time Rayleigh was described in the Certificate of Chancery as 'a very great and populous town having it about three hundred housling people and far from the church'. In 1338 the village was granted to Philippa, wife of Edward III. She erected a court-house but the villagers demolished it. Her removal of a wooden hut from the castle mound and its subsequent re-erection as a hunting lodge in Rayleigh Park was more successfully received. In 1340, the manor was granted by Edward III to William de Bohun, Earl of Northampton, Essex and Hereford. The Earl of Oxford was granted for life (from 1380 to 1400) 'the honor, fee, fair and market of Rayleigh, with the profits of the herbage of Rayleigh Park', and shortly afterwards it was granted to the Duke of York who was killed at Agincourt. In the 16th and 17th centuries Rayleigh was held by the Rich family.

We do not know if King William visited Rayleigh during his reign, but King John had a residence nearby, and visited the village in 1214. In 1449 Henry VI granted the site of a chapel, four acres of land on East Wood, to his loyal subjects. Deer from Rayleigh were introduced into royal parks, and in January 1530 Henry VIII's privy purse expenses included the item: 'the sameday paid one that thought quick der pro Rayleigh for the replenish Greenwich park'. One of Henry's wives, Anne Boleyn, was courted by the king at Rayleigh, making a short journey from Rochford Hall. Queen Elizabeth I was probably the last monarch to follow the hunt in Rayleigh Park.

Swein's Castle at Rayleigh

In 1066, at the time of the Norman invasion, castles were of wooden construction. The castle at Clavering in Essex was built by Robert FitzWimarc, a wealthy Norman at the court of Edward the Confessor. Robert was the father of Swein, the builder of Rayleigh Castle. Swein was probably born in Essex and his castle is the only Essex castle mentioned in Domesday Book: 'In hoc manerio fecit Suenus suum castellum'–'and in this manor Swein has built his castle'.

Rayleigh Castle was built about 1070 under royal licence. The motte and surrounding earthworks would have been raised from earth excavated when digging the moat with the forced labour of local craftsmen. It was a formidable stone stronghold, well defended and constantly enlarged or altered by Swein and his descendants. Swein also cultivated a prosperous vineyard, possibly to the south-east of the castle. The castle occupied a small promontory at the north-west end of the line of Rayleigh Hills, some 200ft. above the low-lying Essex plains, an ideal defensive site for a motte and bailey castle. On the motte, the highest point, stood a lookout tower with the main hall below. The inner bailey contained quarters for Swein's fighting men and a blacksmith, armoury and bakery. The whole, enclosed by a ditch and rampart, covered about four acres. A large outer bailey extended to Bellingham Lane.

After the arrival of the Normans, pockets of English resistance remained. In Essex, FitzWimarc at Clavering and Swein at Rayleigh helped keep the peace and were suitably rewarded. Both held the office of Sheriff of Essex and possibly also of Hertfordshire. Swein held land as tenant-in-chief in no fewer than 15 hundreds, the bulk in the Rochford and neighbouring Barnstable hundreds, ranking the third richest landowner in the area, with an annual income equivalent today (1991) to some £250,000.

Swein was a powerful leader of armed followers and the size, shape and early fortifications of his castle show the potential for harsh authority to be exercised when necessary. He was a great man in his locality, administering his manor and honour from Rayleigh, adding the vigour, wealth and discipline of the Normans to an Anglo-Saxon infrastructure, thus establishing the roots of today's local government.

The disgrace incurred by Swein's grandson, Henry de Essex, resulted in the confiscation of his estates and the family influence declined. With England settled and government more centralised, the castle was no longer required. All that now remain are the sadly overgrown motte and bailey, reminders of the castle's former importance in the Norman settlement of England.

Religion and the Churches

When St Augustine came from Rome in 597 he sent his companion Bishop Mellitus to spread the gospel to the East Saxons. He was driven out and the East Saxons remained pagan until St Cedd, a monk of Lindisfarne in Northumbria, visited them as a missionary bishop in 653. It was he who built St Peter on-the-wall at Bradwell juxta Mare, the first of many churches to be built in Saxon Essex. The first church was built in Rayleigh c.1100, while the present Holy Trinity was erected between 1380 and 1400 on the same site. Built of Kentish ragstone, it is mainly in the perpendicular style with traces of both Norman and Roman masonry. It is believed that de Vere, Earl of Oxford, financed the erection of the tower when he was Lord of the Manor (1380-1400), and Richard II granted the remains of Swein's castle to the inhabitants of Rayleigh in about 1394; as they 'have the will to repair a certain chapel in the said town and to build anew a certain belfry. We have granted them the foundations of a certain old castle which used to be in the town and to take away and use any stones found therein'. The oldest inscription in the church is dated 1416, but there is a mutilated altar tomb which is thought to date from the 12th-14th centuries, though the inscription is gone. A tomb under the arch between the chancel and north aisle is defaced, but some shields remain, with the arms of Barrington. There was once a chantry chapel, but its founder is unknown.

Abraham Caley, rector of Rayleigh from 1643 to 1663, was a puritanical man of the cloth. Twice ejected from the Church, favouring the episcopal form of worship, the Act of Uniformity meant that he underwent much hardship before becoming a founder of the Congregational Church (now the United Reformed), and the Sunday School building on Crown Hill is named after him. He is also said to have held prayer meetings in Meeting House Lane, now Castle Road, after his ejection from the Church in 1662. When Caley died in 1672, Lady Rich of Rochford was 'much moved over the loss of so good a saint and friend'.

There can be little doubt that one of the most influential and respected religious leaders was the Rev. James Pilkington who formed a Baptist congregation in 1797, in spite of considerable opposition. Rayleigh was then considered 'a desolate den of iniquity', with fighting in the streets, but Pilkington built his chapel in 1798-9, and when he first preached the parish church was almost deserted. In 1836 the Baptist chapel was recorded as the only 'dissenting' one in the village. Mr. Pilkington lived in the property which later housed Miss Abbott's school and was adjacent to the present Salvation Army citadel. He died there in 1853 and his body was laid to rest in the graveyard of his own chapel, the Pilkington Memorial Baptist church.

James Banyard (1800-63) was the founder of the 'Peculiar People' sect, which built up a very strong following in this part of Essex. Often misunderstood, the word 'peculiar' meant 'chosen'. It was taken from the Bible: 'Jesus Christ gave himself for us that he might redeem us from all iniquity and purify unto himself a peculiar people, zealous of all good works' (Titus 2:14). Starting in Bellingham Lane they built their own church in Eastwood Road, which is now known as the Evangelical church.

The Methodists now meet in an attractive church in Eastwood Road but their original church, built in 1884, was at the corner of Love Lane and is now occupied by the Salvation Army. The stone-laying ceremony of the new church in 1934 was a splendid event. Fifty stones were laid, of which 30 were in memory of well-known Rayleigh people, including the Rev. Nehemiah Curnock, Mr. Gilson, Mr. Frost and Mr. and Mrs. Priestley, parents of the well-known organist Donald. This was followed by a public tea at the Clissold Hall opposite.

His Lordship, the Bishop of Brentwood, opened 'Our Lady of Ransom' Catholic Church on London Hill on 24 September 1934. It is built in red and gold brick, in Romanesque style.

Education

Education used to depend upon the Church and generous local gentry. Poor children were lucky to learn the 'three Rs' while wealthy families sent their children to boarding establishments. Earliest attempts in Rayleigh to educate the poor were made reputedly by the rectors of Holy Trinity, with boys studying in the porch. On 9 June 1640, Isaac Gilbert left the wherewithal to educate six children; in 1678 James II granted the Rev. John Duff a licence 'to keep one or more schools ... to take boarders in the teachings and instruction of youth'. The Rev. George Sykes (1757-66) left £200 'to learn to write and cast accounts for the boys and, for the girls, so far only as to do plain work ... not to make them useless by interfering with them working'. In 1792 the churchwardens and overseers borrowed £75 from the Rev. Miles Moor to build a new school room and, at about the same time, the Rev. James Pilkington opened Rayleigh Preparatory School as a 'Classical and Commercial School'. The next principal was Robert Henson, uncle of Leslie Henson, a famous comedian in the mid-20th century. In 1839 a boys' school was opened in the grounds of Holy Trinity church where the old schoolroom once stood. The headmaster, a Mr. Bell, later became postmaster. This school was rebuilt in 1870 at a cost of £500, and became the first National School for boys, and then the Parish Rooms. In 1875 there were 90 boys attending, and the fee per day was one penny. A school had been built next to the Baptist chapel in 1863-4, which first taught boys, then became the British School for girls. The first Council school was also the first to mix children; built in Love Lane in 1895, it accepted 72 infants. One can see today where the children sharpened their slate pencils on the brickwork outside. In 1904 a boys' school was built alongside, and soon after a third block, into which the boys moved to make way for the girls and junior children.

By the 1930s, an increasing number of children led to the erection of temporary buildings in the playground, and pupils were bussed to other buildings in or near the town. The new secondary school, later to be called FitzWimarc, was built on Hockley Road in August 1937 at a cost of £26,838. This was followed by several other schools as Rayleigh speedily expanded.

The Workhouse

In 1640 Isaac Gilbert left £6 a year from two tenements for the schooling of poor children in Rayleigh. However, c.1730 these were given up to the parish, and his properties were used as a workhouse until 1836. In 1796 John Pearson agreed to 'find the paupers the necessary meat, drink and clothing ... and to keep, work and employ in a reasonable manner ... and to be allowed 3s. 0d. per week per pauper'. At this time there were 12 aged men, 9 aged women, three girls and three boys resident. Legal steps were taken to check the able-bodied from posing as paupers: a first offence was punished by whipping; the second by cropping of the ears; the third by the death sentence. Later the law changed, and offenders were branded with a 'V'. In 1836 the workhouse was demolished.

Local Government

From 1894 Rayleigh had a parish council, and the main local services were administered by the Rochford Rural District Council. The main administrative offices were in the village of Rochford some six miles from Rayleigh. In 1929, however, by an order made by the Minister of Health, the parishes of Rayleigh and Rawreth were combined to form the Urban District of Rayleigh, with an operational date from 1 January 1930. The Urban District Council established its offices at 28 High Street at a large detached house (the site is now occupied by Woolworth's), and one of its first tasks was to provide an efficient sewerage and sewage disposal scheme. This was done by means of a 75 per cent government grant, which was made on the understanding that 75 per cent of the Council's workforce was drawn from the ranks of the unemployed. The fire service was updated by the purchase of a new fire engine, street lighting was improved and active steps were taken to make up the many private streets in the area which were practically impassable to traffic during inclement weather. The new council consisted of 18 members (12 from Rayleigh and six from Rawreth) but this proportion was subsequently changed in order to reflect the very substantial increase in the population of Rayleigh. The first chairman was Ernest P. Rand, a local horticulturist, who had served on the parish council for many years and was instrumental in obtaining urban powers for the area. The population of the new district was 5,840, and when the urban district ceased to exist after local government reorganisation in 1974, this had increased to around 30,000. Very rapid development had taken place in the intervening years. Open spaces and playing fields were provided, including an area in the centre of Rayleigh known as Webster's Meadow (now King George's field) where provision was made for football, cricket and bowls.

The early years of the new council were somewhat hampered by the threat of war during the latter part of the 1930s, when time and effort had to be devoted to the preparation of emergency services. After the war the council resumed its activities in earnest, and services were updated. The old Rayleigh mill buildings were purchased to provide a new leisure centre; a substantial public hall (Rayleigh Mill Hall) was built; new municipal housing schemes were inaugurated; and new administrative offices were obtained by the conversion of an old manor house known as 'Barringtons', where new offices and a modern council chamber were constructed.

Rayleigh Windmill

Approaching Rayleigh from Rawreth one can see two outstanding landmarks, Holy Trinity Church and Rayleigh's tower mill. The mill stands on the outer bailey of the old Rayleigh Castle from where it can be seen for several miles. It is brick with a wooden housing, fan tail and sail, and was built about 1798. For many years after 1906 it was without sails, but these were replaced in 1974 complete with new housing and fantail. The money was raised for this by the well-known benefactor Mr. R. T. Byford, public subscription and a grant from the council. 1989 saw the gantry replaced, returning the mill to its former glory. Rayleigh Windmill had many owners, one of the earliest being Benjamin Ruffles (who also owned another mill on the Hockley Road near FitzWimarc School, called Ruffles Mill). It was another owner, Mr. Brown who had the sails taken down in 1906, because the miller, Mr. Crabb, became too old to tend them; it had been a very tiring 24-hour job and nobody could be found to take over. Steam was then brought into use and later a diesel engine. Mr. White, who at one time worked at the mill, remembers delivering loads as far away as Bicknacre, crossing the river by the old ford at Hullbridge. There are two sad stories attached to the mill. One workman fell 30 ft. when taking down the sails in 1906, breaking his thigh. Even more tragic was the murder of Mr. Brown by his son in 1943. Mr. Brown, owner at that time, was a very unhappy invalid, and in July 1943, one son, who was in the army, placed a grenade mine under the cushions of his father's invalid chair and Nurse Mitchell, who took him for walks, pushed him along Hockley Road for his usual outing. Mr. Brown wanted a cigarette so the nurse helped him to light it. As they continued the walk the invalid shifted in his chair, the mine exploded and Nurse Mitchell was knocked unconscious. The explosion killed the patient as well as seriously injuring his attendant.

In 1970 the mill was leased for a peppercorn rent from the Rayleigh Council by the Rayleigh Antiquarian and Natural History Society. They now run it as a small museum. Unfortunately it has a ladder-backed staircase so the upper floors are not open to the public. Many of the exhibits are from the Rayleigh area and photographs of past and present residents are displayed. The Society is also responsible for six plaques seen around Rayleigh. These were made by the boys at Rayleigh Sweyne Comprehensive School with the help of Mr. Jack Cooper, head of the Handiwork Department. They commemorate the Annual Fair in the High Street; the outer bailey of Rayleigh Castle; Barringtons and Kingsley house; the house of Mr. E. B. Francis, who donated the Mount; and Pilkington's School, one of the earliest schools in Rayleigh. At present the mill is open each Saturday morning between April and September and manned by voluntary members of the Society.

Transport

Until the late 19th century the main road from London to Prittlewell came up to London Hill, through the High Street and then via Two Mill Lane, later Mill Lane, Eastwood Lane and now Eastwood Road. It continued through Eastwoodbury, past where the airport is today and then up Prittlewell Hill. Before the arrival of motor transport, coaches would call at the hostelries where horses were changed and travellers rested. Coaching inns, with arches to the stables behind, included the *Golden Lion*, a major coach stop, and the *Chequers*, which had its own smithy within living memory. It is said that Lord Rich (1500-68) was often seen pasing through the village with a coach and six outriders. *The Crown* was a staging post for coaches running from Aldgate to Prittlewell, and a wagonette left there for Benfleet Station to collect newspapers before the coming of the railway to Rayleigh. A shrimp coach, carrying both passengers and fish, started in Leigh and passed through Rayleigh on the way to the market in London. Much of the produce from local farms was conveyed by horse and cart. A carrier known as 'Uncle' Brand lived in a cottage opposite where the public library is today, and travelled between Rayleigh and Chelmsford twice a week with supplies. Many farm animals continued to be moved on foot from and to Canvey, Wickford and even Chelmsford.

Before the arrival of buses Rayleigh was well served with taxis, and it was not until 1921 that the Westcliff-on-Sea Motor Services began a passenger service from Rayleigh to Southend, via Eastwood, and in 1923 a route via Hadleigh. These vehicles had open top decks, open stairways and open cabs. The drivers wore cap and goggles, and sheltered behind a canvas cover. As the years passed by so the competition increased, and the bus services improved. A bus ran *c.*1926 from the London area to Southend through Romford, Billericay and Rayleigh, and other services to Chelmsford and Clacton were added later.

Most tradesmen continued for several years with horse-drawn carts because of the unmade roads which made many impossible to negotiate during the winter months. So we saw the baker sitting high on his box cart, the milkman in blue and white striped apron mounted behind his gleaming milk churn as if driving a chariot, the oilman with his sturdy horse and well-laden cart and the coalman with his sweating horses and smiling, blackened face.

The Brewery, Inns and Taverns

The brewery, demolished in 1922, was situated in the High Street opposite Eastwood Road and Dolmartons, in the area now occupied by Dairy Crest and the frontage shops. Before Harry Luker took over in 1885 it was run by a Mr. Woolston who had learnt his trade at the City of London Brewery. Luker's drew some of their water from the brickfield pond in Castle Road until a body was found floating there. It was not the kind of body required in the brew, so the business was transferred to Southend.

Rayleigh has always been well served with hostelries and within living memory there have been at least eleven. The *Bull* (1560-1791) has been replaced long since by Kingsleigh House, first a private school and now solicitors' offices. Bull-baiting once took place there in the yard at the back. The *Golden Lion* ceased trading in 1930, while in Hockley Road were the *Five Bells* and the *Drovers' Arms*. *Chequers* in the High Street, with its sombre frontage but intriguing archway leading to a smithy and cottages behind, gave way to shop development. Near the corner of Meeting House Lane, now Castle Road, were the *Elephant and Castle* and the *Plough*, with the former on the south side and the latter approximately where the police car pound is today. The *Bricklayers Arms* in Trenders Avenue, Rawreth, still stands but no longer trades. In spite of these losses there still remain several historic public houses, each of which has adapted to the many changes in the trade. Roughly from the north to south they are the *Half Moon*, *White Horse*, *Crown*, *Spread Eagle* and *Paul Pry*. Opened c.1924 was the *Weir*, which took the licence of the Elephant when it was demolished.

The War Years

During the early part of the First World War, enlisting stations were opened locally and much of the youth of the district volunteered. Many lost their lives serving the country, and their names are recorded on memorial tablets in the parish church, and at the British Legion memorial hall on London Hill. A feature of the war was the billeting of large numbers of army units, some being from the 16th King's Royal Rifles in the area. A home defence corps was formed by local volunteers; daily newspapers, cigarettes and tobacco were sold to men from the canteen in the parish room under special government licence. Being in direct line from the continent to London a number of zeppelins and aeroplanes were seen over the village, some of which jettisoned bombs on the countryside, particularly when being chased home. A stained glass window dedicated to the armistice was erected in the chancel of the parish church.

The Second World War saw Rayleigh classified as a 'Neutral Area': residents were not evacuated nor did the area receive official evacuees, although some displaced children were cared for by local families, and many people, made homeless from enemy action in the London area, came to the village for shelter. Emergency civil defence services were organised and a local defence volunteer force, later known as the Home Guard, was established. An air training corps and women's junior air corps were also set up while searchlights and anti-aircraft units were stationed here.

Rayleigh, because of its proximity to London, witnessed a number of aerial combats, and bombs were dropped in the district. The village also suffered badly from the effects of both the enemy V1, an unmanned high-explosive bomb driven by a small engine, and the V2, a massive high-explosive projectile fired from across the channel. Some people were killed, many others were injured and much damage was caused to property. A local invasion committee with power to control all civil matters should the district become isolated was established in 1940. A lych-gate outside the parish church was erected, as a result of public subscription, to commemorate the fallen.

Bibliography

Addison, W., *Essex Worthies*, 1973.
Benton, P., *History of Rochford Hundred*, 1880.
Coller, D. W., *People's History of Essex*, 1861.
Edwards, A. C., *A History of Essex*, 1978.
Emmison, F. G., *Elizabethan Life and Disorder*, 1964.
Fryer, Rev. A. G., *Rayleigh in Past Days*, 1908.
Jerram-Burrows, L. E., *Bygone Rochford*, 1988.
Morant, P., *Historical and Geological History of Rochford Hundred*, 1768.
Norden, J., *Description of the County of Essex*, 1594.
Pollitt, W., *The Archaeology of Rochford Hundred*, 1935.
Pusey, R., *A Discovery of Essex*, 1985.
Rayleigh Civic Society, *Historical Guides*, various.
Rayleigh and District Antiquarian and Natural History Society, various.
Scott, E. V., *The Best of Essex Countryside*, 1976.

1. Grant of Arms to the former Urban District Council of Rayleigh. Letters patent granting and assigning Armorial Bearings to the Council was approved on 20 December 1962 by the College of Arms. The Latin means 'We work for the future'.

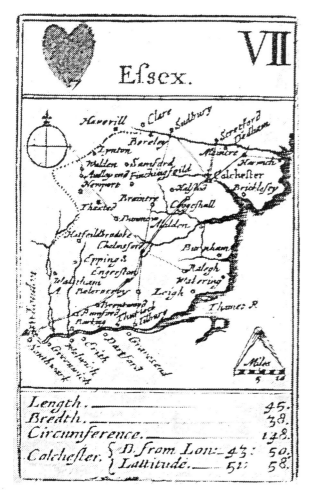

2. The first pocket atlas of Essex. Over 300 years ago there were 52 counties – the same number as playing cards in a pack. When this coincidence was realised, cardmakers prepared packs with a county map on each card, this covering the principal roads, rivers and towns of the whole country. The card chosen for Essex was the seven of hearts, which showed 'Ralegh'.

3. To celebrate Essex Heritage Year in 1989, Rayleigh Civic Society donated this town sign, now erected on the corner of the High Street and Bellingham Lane. Cast in aluminium and hand painted, it displays four scenes of Rayleigh: the parish church, the windmill, the Dutch Cottage and Rayleigh Mount.

4. Holy Trinity church, showing the ivy which covered the building until major restoration works were carried out in 1912.

5.   The interior of Holy Trinity church, *c*.1922, before the erection of the rood screen. The stained-glass windows in the Sanctuary were erected in 1921 as a thank-offering for the restoration of peace, following the First World War.

6.   The 1912 restoration in progress at Holy Trinity church.

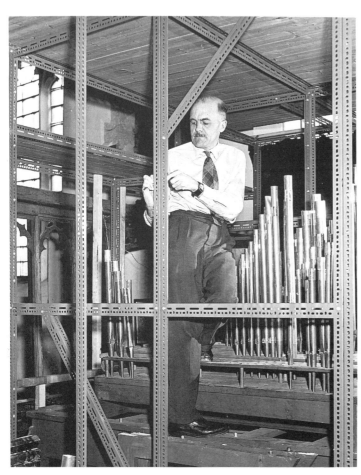

7. The late Mr. Ken Cotton, former organist at the parish church, seen here rebuilding the organ in 1966. He incorporated a Compton cinema organ from the Pavilion cinema, Reading, and electrified the action.

8. Rayleigh High Street, *c*.1900, looking towards the parish church.

9. View from Church Street *c.*1930, showing the *Golden Lion*, which was demolished *c.*1950. Keeble's sold newspapers on Sunday and during the week Mr. Keeble also sold shellfish and shrimps from a basket.

10. Patmore's baker's shop was the location of the first telephone exchange, *c.*1920. A call took precedence over a customer buying at the counter. Bowen's is in Church Street, and the property to the left is Mr. Toes' dentistry.

11.   Bowen's second shop was a temporary arrangement. Before it was opened, the lean-to was owned by Herbert Smith who let it out, *c*.1900, to a Reading and Dramatic Club. At one time billiards was played there.

12.   Arthur Ager at his shop door *c*.1910 waiting, no doubt, for the approaching family to enter. Next door are the bill boards of Miss Judd's newsagents.

13. The High Street, *c.*1900, showing Mr. Ratty Cook's shoe shop, one of the oldest cottages in existence today, dating from the 16th century or earlier.

14. High Street. This old photograph, date unknown, was taken before both Patmore's and Ager's opened. The former's premises were occupied by Mr. Pease who sold flour, corn, hay and straw, while Mr. Ager's shop was Dixon's.

15. A woman who lived in Rayleigh, and a supporter of the suffragette movement, was thought to be responsible for this damage to the Post Office, c.1912.

16. *White Horse Inn, c.*1900.

17. Swein's Castle as it might have appeared in the 12th century, by Alan Sorrell, who was an associate of the Royal College of Art and was awarded the Prix de Roma for mural painting. His works appear in most leading galleries in London, including the Tate.

18.   The staff of H. Mann and Son, the grocer's shop in the High Street, are joined by Manny Stewart, the saddler, young Harry Mann, later 2nd Rayleigh Troop Scoutmaster, and Bert Cottee, who subsequently opened his own grocer's shop. Miss Ford, who for many years kept the books, stands at the entrance. The photograph dates from 1920.

19. Eastwood Lodge was first recorded in 1210. Its name was taken from the east wood of Rayleigh, and passed to the De Eastwood family. It is now occupied by the aged persons of the Field Lane Foundation.

20. This photograph was taken c.1925, when buses would turn in the centre of the village to wait either at the *Crown* or at Frost's, where tea was available for the crews.

21. The girls of Bellingham House School in Bellingham Lane prepare for tennis. Note the airy, light classrooms and the smartness of the girls.

22. Mr. S. Brewer, a local baker, traded from this shop *c*.1925 and then sold the premises in 1935 to Cottis and Sons, who continued to trade as bakers.

23. Colvin and Hinksman's garage in the High Street, which sold Guaranteed No. 1 petrol at 1s. 1d. a gallon. Later, *c*.1930, the partnership split, and Mr. Hinksman crossed the road to the Crown Garage. During the '30s, the pavements and kerbs were improved.

24. Chequers Yard, *c.*1890. This photograph shows Mr. Richardson's forge, with the owner in the centre. The White, Rollingson and Dykes families lived in the cottages at this time.

25. Chequers Yard. Another view of the forge, taken on the same day as the preceding picture.

26. The 'Wigwam', *c*.1910, the right-hand cottage, was the base for 1st Rayleigh Scouts. After the First World War the Scouts and Cubs met in an old army hut in Love Lane. A smaller hut now stands on the same site.

27. A recurring problem was the flooding of the High Street, as the open ditches could not cope with heavy rain or sudden thaw. The picture was taken in 1910.

28. Mr. Stewart, the harness maker, about to set off on his motor-bike, *c.*1920. His wife is riding pillion and his father is in the side-car.

29. Mr. Stewart outside his shop, *c*.1930, which was replaced first by Sadler's Restaurant and later by McKays. From time to time shining leather and gleaming harnesses were hung outside as horses and carts drew up for measuring and fitting.

30. Rayleigh High Street before the martyrs' memorial was erected in 1908.

31. Times are changing, *c.*1922, with not a horse in sight, but business at the Crown garage grows daily.

32. Village centre looking south, *c.*1910.

33.   The tranquil village centre in 1890.

34.   The High Street, looking towards Luker's Brewery, c.1910. The home of E. B. Francis, now Lloyds Bank, is on the right.

35. Martin Tweed and his wife proudly pose before the tea rooms, which were taken down in 1925 for the Crown Hill widening. The picture shows that soda or milk is 1½d. a glass.

36. Mr. Olley, who kept the bicycle shop in the village centre, also made boots, while Mr. Upson worked behind his wife's greengrocery shop. He made harnesses, one of which hangs on the wall. The picture was taken *c.*1910.

37. This photograph shows Westminster Bank, which took over Olley's shop, and is now Leeds Permanent Building Society. This picture was taken in 1934.

38. A. J. Barnard's house and off licence, *c.*1930. There is a delivery van outside and a poster on the fence advertising a carnival and sports, to be held on Websters Meadow. Today the site is occupied by Superdrug, and the sideway leads to the Dairy Crest depot.

39. The demolition of Luker's Brewery, situated opposite Eastwood Road, in 1922. The children are on their way to nearby Love Lane school.

40. Barnett's the bakers with Mrs. Barnett and her two daughters, *c.*1905. The delivery lads proudly wait with their horses and traps before making their rounds.

41. Fred Dawes pauses while on his rounds delivering bread, *c.*1923. This type of cart was necessary as the roads were unmade.

42. When Devison's, the haberdashers, and Westminster Bank left this 14th-century building in the 1930s, it became the gas showroom. Now Sansoms have tastefully refurbished it in Georgian style.

43. Outside Davies' chemist's shop, *c*.1910. Devison's the drapers and Davies' the chemists, are both visible in what is now Rayleigh Lanes.

44. Gilson's, the grocer's shop, *c.*1920, was in the High Street where Dorothy Perkins is today.

45. High Street, *c.*1900, before the martyrs' memorial had been erected.

46. Mr. Cook outside Frost's, which started as a hatter's shop, but later became a confectioner, tobacconist and tea room.

47. This fine old boneshaker, a Dennis, was an advance on the open-cabbed buses which were used earlier. Standing in Rayleigh High Street in 1924, the vehicle was destined for Southend.

48. This is how ladies of fashion would have looked in Rayleigh during Edwardian times. From left to right: Mrs. May Norton (from whose collection the garments came), Edna Simmons and May's daughter, Judy Lawrence.

49. In 1900 trees were planted in the High Street, before the erection of the memorial, which took place in 1908.

50. 'The noble army of martyrs'. Thus begins the inscription on the monument erected in the High Street in memory of Thomas Causton, burned on this spot on 17 March 1555, and others who suffered. When the site was levelled for the monument it was said a burned stake was found in the ground.

51.   A busy High Street, *c*.1890.

52.   Trinity fair in the High Street, with not a single bare head in sight. This was a grand annual event from 1227 to the late 1880s, when it was moved to Webster's Meadow. The special day was August bank holiday – the first Monday of the month – when the carnival procession was held.

53.   The fair was a great attraction for gypsies, who set up their shies and games.

54. Aunt Sally at Rayleigh
Trinity Fair, *c.*1890.

55. Rayleigh Fair, *c*.1898.

56.   The Zulu about to join the carnival procession in 1934,
Mr. E. H. 'Ernie' Lane, was later to organise the last carnival
held in Rayleigh.

57.   There was warm sunshine for the 1921 carnival as is
evident by the group under the scant shade of the tree. The
lady with the pram is Mrs. Arthur Ager.

58. The mill, *c.*1900, complete and working. It is now Rayleigh Museum, situated behind the Mill Hall.

59. Great Wheatley, (from hweate-leah, a wheat clearing) was mentioned in Domesday as a farm. Given to the abbey by Robert, son of Swein, for his 'souls sake', it became a manor *c.*1300. The present building dates partly from the 16th and 18th centuries. The east wing was added later.

60. Mr. Keys, the corn chandler, *c*.1925, delivering in the village. In those days most families had big gardens, kept chickens and grew most of their own vegetables and fruit.

61. Castle Road, c.1880.

62. The Brickfield pond off Castle Road c.1925, now a refuse disposal site and private development. Once a favourite spot for fishermen under licence from the Council, it was also the main source of water for Luker's Brewery.

63. Mr. and Mrs. William Flick of Castle Road with daughters Lily and Maudie, and two soldiers who were billeted with the family in 1914.

64. A letter, sent by one of the soldiers in France in 1916, arrived safely in spite of the brief address.

65.   King's Royal Rifles. The General's parade in the village centre in 1915. Every household had to billet two soldiers during the First World War.

66. Rayleigh men who fought in the First World War.

67. On the north side of the railway between Rayleigh and Wickford there is a grave which marks the spot where two British pilots collided in mid-air on 7 March 1918, after pursuing German raiders. It is to the memory of Captain H. C. Stroud R.F.C., and nearby is the second grave to the memory of Captain Bruce Kynoch R.F.C.

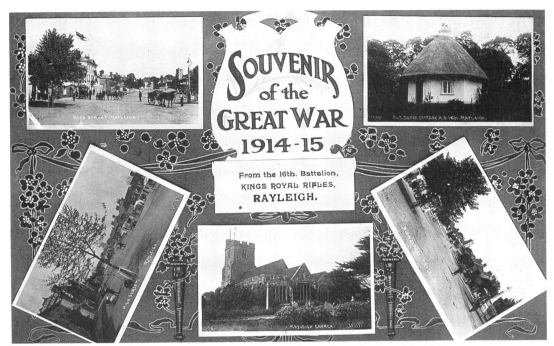

68. A souvenir postcard from Rayleigh, dating from the First World War.

69. It is not known whether these airship parts passing through Rayleigh *c.*1918 were from the wreck of the zeppelin which fell at Billericay or are new parts for a British one. In support of the latter theory, the engine and fabric appear undamaged.

70.   Peace Day parade to mark the end of the First World War, passing through the High Street. A Union Jack flies outside the old post office.

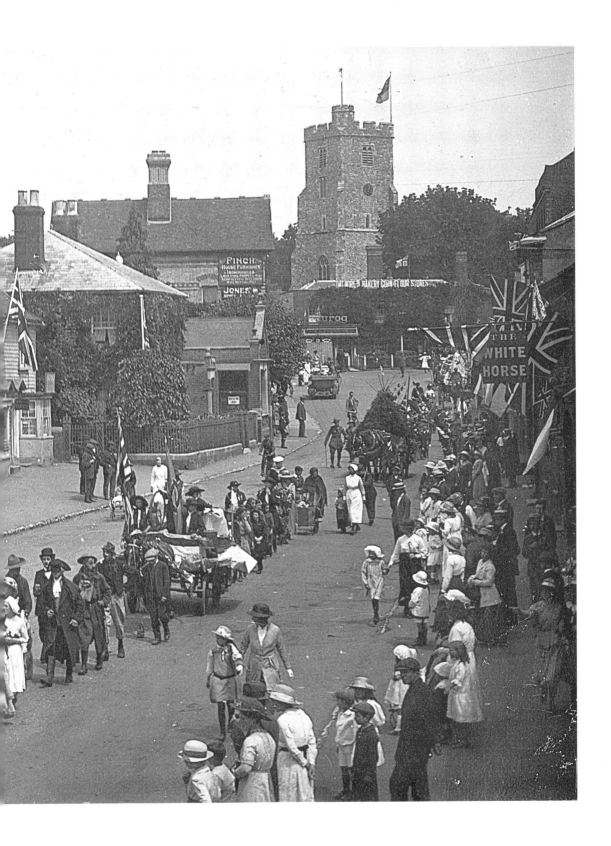

71. Sergeant Gentry, in charge of the police at the turn of the century, operated from his cottage in Eastwood Road. On retirement, the police released the rented property to the owners so he could continue to live there. Sergeant Alders succeeded him at the small station on the corner of High Street and Eastwood Road, now occupied by a florist.

72. HJ 7334, a Gilford 26-seater. This service, from Rayleigh to Southend, started 7 December 1927 and the following year another Gilford 32-seater and a Tilling ran every half hour from Rayleigh Chase to the L.N.E.R.'s station at Southend.

73. Rayleigh Town Band, *c.*1918. Walter Griffin was bandmaster.

74. A typical milk cart which was in use locally well into the 20th century. The brass milkchurn was always highly polished, and the milkmen dispensed milk with a ladle into jugs.

75. The W. H. Flack entry in the carnival on Webster's Meadow, *c*.1925, with Gerald Flack on the cart. W. H. Flack is next to the cart, and his father is wearing the bowler.

76. This delightful picture was taken at the horticultural show in 1901.

77. A gift of £18,000 in 1952 by a local resident, Mr. T. W. Finch and his sister, Mrs. E. J. Seed, provided the 12 Finchfield Trust bungalows on Eastwood Road. They are for residents who have lived in the district for at least 30 years, and are over sixty-five.

78. A charabanc outing approaches Eastwood Road corner. A taxi stands outside the *Spread Eagle*. Built *c*.1500, trading commenced at the inn about 150 years ago.

79. Barringtons was home of John de Barenton, Keeper of the Royal Park, who died in 1416, and is remembered in Holy Trinity by a stone slab bearing mutilated effigies of him and his wife, Thomasina. The house was rebuilt in 1844 by Daniel Nash and named Rayleigh Place, but there has since been a return to the old name of Barringtons.

80. Rawreth Lane, *c*.1925.

81. Wickford Road, *c*.1880, looking towards Rayleigh parish church, mill and mount. The lady with the buckets has a hoop-like fitment to protect her legs.

82. Mr. and Mrs. Olley leave to take part in the 1921 carnival, on a unique side-by-side machine built by Mr. Olley.

83. The stage-coach to London about to leave the *Crown*, *c.*1885.

84. The annual horse market, *c.*1890, before it moved to Webster's Meadow. Caravans at the *Crown* suggest gypsy involvement.

85. The meet, pictured here *c.*1908, foregathered for many years at the *Crown*. With so much open, green country nearby a good day's sport was assured.

86. Rayleigh High Street, *c*.1910.

87. Boys of the National School, *c*.1900.

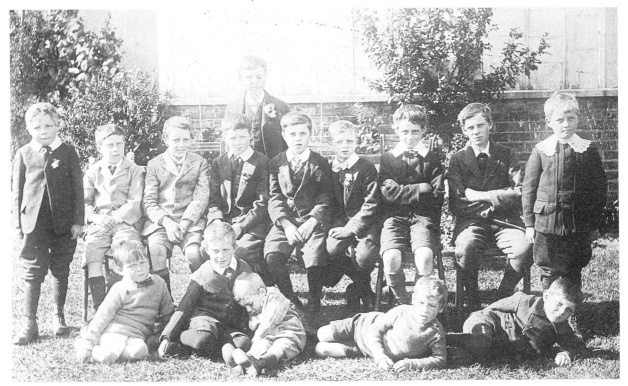

88. Rayleigh High Street in the late 1880s.

89 & 90. Two buses on the Rayleigh to Southend route, which commenced in 1923. The Southend bus is standing outside Barnett's the bakers, near the Martyr's Memorial. The other waits by the *Crown*.

91.   The forge alongside Dollmartons, photographed *c*.1890, fronted an open field, part of Hog Farm which ran along Mill Lane, now Eastwood Road. The farmhouse was Peveril's, which later became the police station.

92.   High Street, *c*.1890. The view is up to Sandpit Cottage in the High Road. Miss Abbott's school is on the right; the long building is Nash's dairy. Castle Road is to the left and Love Lane to the right.

93. Miss Abbott's school, High Street. The Rev. J. Pilkington, Baptist minister and campaigner against slavery, lived here, *c.*1850.

94. These cottages, once opposite the present library in the High Street, are decorated for the Coronation of King George VI in 1937.

95. The Wesleyan church at the corner of Love Lane was built in 1885, and the Sunday School in 1902. On 11 May 1935 the Salvation Army, which had formed in 1923, sold their hall (now the Women's Institute Hall) and purchased the church and school for £2,000. Repairs and decorations by Bartlet Tregenza cost an additional £325.

96. Miss Mercy Mary Smith's general store, once situated opposite the Baptist church, sold everything from paraffin to bullseyes. The eccentric Miss Smith allowed a rabbit to run free in the shop.

97. The *Elephant and Castle* at the corner of Castle Road, *c*.1900, from a painting by the landlord, Mr. Fidgeon.

98. In 1798-9 Pilkington Memorial Chapel was built in the High Road by the Rev. James Pilkington, who was Rayleigh's first non-conformist clergyman.

99.   Children in their Sunday best depart from the Baptist chapel, which was next to the school for girls, the British School, High Road. Love Lane school took over in 1906.

100.   British School, High Road, *c*.1907.

101.   Looking west across the valley towards Wickford from the corner of High Road and Ridgeway, *c.*1925.

102.   Formerly Britton's farmhouse, Sandpit Cottage was demolished *c.*1950 and was on the site of 172 High Street.

103. Albert French, landlord of the *Paul Pry* tavern in the High Road, *c.*1914, with his sons Len and Reg, both of whom became school teachers.

104. The *Paul Pry* was named after a character in a comedy written by John Poole and produced in 1825 at the Haymarket. The centre of the building is about 350 years old and the front elevation has hardly changed from when it was first built. In more recent times, coffins were made in the front barn and quoits was played where cars are now parked.

105. Looking towards Rayleigh from the weir, with the garage of Mr. A. J. Springett in view. He pioneered an early bus route in the 1930s, from Rayleigh to Rochford, Southend, Hadleigh and back to Rayleigh. Small single-decker buses were used.

106. By the weir pond, 1915.

107. Prince Henry of Gloucester may not have realised when opening the Rayleigh section of the first purpose-built arterial road, the A127, in 1923, that so many other royal figures had been to the area before him. The village turned out in strength to mark the event.

108. The first lane of the A127 was cut through by hand. Spoil was moved on a narrow-gauge railway to make up lower levels. Enterprise was shown by Albert French of the *Paul Pry* who supplied drinks and light refreshment to the workforce, while Harding's, once sausage-makers of Bull Lane, sold ice cream.

109. Weir Corner, in the 1920s, in the days when the A.A. man would stand in the centre saluting his members. A flashing beacon stood nearby when the A127 was first opened, to warn Rayleigh and Thundersley motorists of the 'speeding' traffic.

110. Albert Baker, seen here *c.*1875, was a hard-working Rayleigh man who built up a prosperous transport business and provided each of his six boys and five girls with houses. Ten of these were built in a row in Claydons Lane. He was a big employer of labour in the district, owning several local farms.

111. The weir pond was frozen over in 1895.

112. A lorry belonging to A. Baker and Sons unloading material for the new London to Southend arterial road in 1923. The company also bussed labourers from distressed areas to and from the station. Another contract involved moving grain and flour from London docks to Rayleigh mill.

113. Love Lane, *c.*1890. The gap to the right led into Hopton's meadow, and from there to Crown Hill.

114. Love Lane, *c.*1958. The cottage still defies the developers. The gas-holders have arrived to relieve the small one on Crown Hill. In the late 19th century the area was called 'Sweetdowns'.

115. A view *c.*1925 from the top of Hoptons meadow at the end of Love Lane, showing Sweeps Row. This was the substantial house of E. M. Goult, an antiquarian with great knowledge of Rayleigh history. The railway cottages through the trees and the kissing gate at the bottom of the footpath can also be seen.

116. Mr. E. B. Francis took this picture from 'Sweetdowns' in 1890. It shows Sweeps Row to the left, Dutch Cottage, Crown Lane and, in the centre, the old pathway to the Mount. Permission from the *Crown Hotel* was needed to pass through the gate. The Baptist Tabernacle, later the Congregational church, had not yet been built.

117.   The infants' school in Love Lane was built in 1895, and was the first mixed school in the village. It had two classrooms.

118.   Playtime at Love Lane infants' school, *c.*1890.

119. Love Lane Boys' School on the opening day in 1909. Mr. Vicars, former head of the National school, was appointed headmaster and is seen with Mr. Stratford, Chairman of Managers, and other local dignitaries.

120. Rayleigh Senior Schoolboys' cup-winning football team seen here in 1933. The teachers are 'Taffy' Sample and Len French; the boys: White, Miller, Harvey, S. Mathews, Phillips, Shelley, R. Harvey, Morgan, Baker, Coker and Wildman.

121. Harry Thorogood's forge in Eastwood Road. There were five other forges in Rayleigh at one time, but Harry's was the last to close, in 1956.

122. The view across Webster's Meadow, *c*.1910. In the distance, below the church, is Barrington's, and the cottages which still stand in Bull Lane.

123.   Eastwood Road, *c*.1920, looking towards the High Street with Webster's Meadow in the distance and the Peculiar People's chapel left of centre.

124. The new Methodist church and Sunday School in Eastwood Road was opened on 7 November 1934. Its first minister was the Rev. Walter Budd. After the opening, members and guests crossed to the Clissold Hall opposite to take tea at 9d. a head.

125. Mill Lane, later Eastwood Road, *c.*1870. The pond is at the corner of Daws Heath Road, and an isolated Picton House is in the centre of the photograph.

126. This charabanc, called Rayleigh Grey, is standing outside its owner's garage, once between Queens Road and Picton House, *c.*1925.

127. Two post mills once stood in Picton House grounds. The first, Great Lodge Mill, was built before 1775, when a sale from Mr. Fairhead, cordwainer, to Nathaniel Audley, miller, was recorded. The second was mentioned in 1793 when insurance cover for a new mill was arranged. Both were dismantled by the end of the last century.

128. Picton House, *c*.1890. Mr. Sparrow, the cobbler, worked in the barn, left, before moving to a tiny shop by the *Spread Eagle*.

129. Eastwood Road, *c*.1920, showing work in progress on a widening scheme near the entrance to Picton House.

130. Trinity Road was made up early this century but the roads to the right and beyond remained unmade until the 1930s. The view, *c*.1925, shows the bend into Grove Road and across open fields towards Hockley.

131. The pond at the corner of White House Chase and Eastwood Road, *c*.1910. White House produced wine for Rayleigh Lodge when Henry VIII entertained Anne Boleyn there, and two windmills stood on the adjacent farm until *c*.1880, not to be confused with those at Picton House.

132. One of the oldest buildings in the village, with much of the original structure remaining, is the White House, dating from the 16th century. The farm once covered hundreds of acres and 120 years ago 14 ploughmen worked the estate. Nearby a pond of some two acres, called 'Fishponds', was formed by the damming of a stream from the royal park. This could have been the 'great pond' referred to by Henry VIII when requesting Sir Anthony Browne to prepare a lawn for 'disport and pleasure'.

133. This little shop was once situated at the corner of The Chase and Eastwood Road, photographed here *c.*1928.

134. Rayleigh Lodge in 1920 had much changed since playing host to Henry VIII and Anne Boleyn.

135.   Leslie Road, *c.*1925. In winter the mud was so deep that horses had to be dug out. Beyond The Chase was scrubland and one or two isolated bungalows.

136. Daws Heath Road at its junction with White House Chase. The large double-fronted house known as 'Silverdale' was demolished in 1961 and a new housing estate known by that name has been erected in its place.

137. Eastwood Road, *c*.1910, looking down Lime House Hill towards Southend. Cramphorns garden centre now occupies the site to the left of the picture.

138.   Eastwood Road, *c.*1921, looking up Lime House Hill. Road repairs are in progress.

139.   Helena Road, 17 April 1943. The explosion of a land mine sadly resulted
in the death of Mrs. Martin, wife of a highly-respected nurseryman. The last V2
to hit Britain fell close to 'Wychwood', Dawsheath Road, opposite Kings Farm.

140. Victoria Road residents turned out for this photograph *c*.1910, when the unmade road had dried out in the summer.

141. 1476 (Rayleigh) Squadron Air Training Corps, formed in 1941, and shown here in 1943. It is estimated that over 200 cadets entered the armed forces between 1941 and 1953. The Squadron did more than train and educate: it helped build character in its members. From left to right: (back row) John Nurding, Brian Jackson, Fred Leeding, Derek Baker, Dennis Bright, Ray Such, Gordon Richardson, Roy Baker, Peter Ashby, George Hudson, Albert Cozens, Brian Beckwith, not known; (third row) Ray Green, not known, Ron Wilkinson, Billy Halls, Dizzy Davis, Bill Lee, Ken Whiting, Peter Golledge, Cyril Sandford, Geoff Keen, Les Brown, not known, Les Grigg, Norman Willson, Bill Castleton; (second row) not known, Michael O'Connell, Geoff Snell, Horace Bourne, W/O Miles Compton, P/O Will Smith, F/O Arthur Palmer, Flt/Lt Len French, P/O Sid Jackson, Colin Denson, Jim Creek, Ray Farnborough, John Turner; (front row) Barrie Faulkner, not known, Barry Baker, Terry Fitzgerald, not known, not known, Jimmy Hillier, Ralph Lake, Stan Hawes, Paul (Pongo) Oates, Ray Stock.

142. The mill from the church tower, *c*.1900, with the railway station on the right, and goods depot on the left. Right of centre are Mount Pleasant cottages. Repairs are taking place on cottages which were later replaced by the Conservative Club. The vacant ground to the right was a Council Depot.

143. Clement White, pictured in 1924. He wrote on the reverse of this card: 'Dear Sir, Allow me to say that in the year 1919 I became head Carman for the well beloved millers Mr. Thos. Brown & Son, for whom I worked for many years and enjoyed every day. Also too, the horsedrawn van was builted by Mr. Witham of Rayleigh, weighing 1t 30cwt'.

144. Mr. Crabb, the last miller to operate the sails of Rayleigh windmill, in 1906.

145. The old Rayleigh rectory, which stood near the site of the present one. It was demolished in 1967 because of its poor structural condition.

146. Barrington's cottages, occupying the site of those built for the royal forest workers, now mark the boundary of the market held each Wednesday near the parish church. The market was first authorised in 1225 by Hubert de Burgh, Justiciar of England.

147.   Bomb damage viewed from Barrington's, on 31 October 1940.

148.   Fern House, Hockley Road, built in the 15th century, is still standing today. Situated near the parish church, it was once a private school.

149.   Hockley Road, before 1920. The cottage, which was being used as a bicycle shop was demolished *c*.1950.

150.   Mr. Ernie Stratford's nurseries stretched from Hockley Road to Bull Lane, covering some nine acres. In the 1960s, Sweyne Court Nursing Home was built on the frontage near the church, while the rest of the land was developed with private housing.

151. The Rev. Nehemiah Curnock, who lived in Cedar Lodge, Hockley Road, and edited the Methodist Recorder, here seen using an early typewriter, *c*.1905. In 1909, the code to John Wesley's Journals was revealed to him in a dream, thus enabling him to publish the journals which had remained undeciphered for 118 years.

152. The *Drover's Arms*, situated in Hockley Road nearly opposite Nelson Road, burned down in 1847 but was rebuilt in 1867. It was much favoured by Hockley men as it stayed open an hour later than Hockley pubs. Miss Bowen, daughter of the landlord, married Mr. Turnridge of Leigh in 1886, and this is their wedding party.

153. 373 (Rayleigh) Squadron Women's Junior Air Corps, formed in 1942, and pictured here in 1943. Left to right: (back row) Yvonne Cox, Pat Carter, Rita Sears, Audrey Murphy, Betty Gould, Jeanette Lofts, Doreen Wilson, Olive Eastaugh, June Harms, Peggy Dowling; (middle row) Trevina Floyd, not known, Joey Stone, Gwen Tratt, Irene Warner, Kitty Draper, Peggy Cripps, not known, Doreen North, Audrey Ibbotsen; (front row) Pat Anderson, Eileen Ward, Cherry Willson, Pat Barker (Adj.), Mrs. M. Jackson (C.O.), Helen Knott (Jn.O.), W/O Miles Compton, Doreen Keegan, Jose Horwood; (kneeling) Bunty Corbell, Pam Holden.

154. To view this scene you would have to be standing outside the present Conservative Club looking towards Church Street. The property facing is still standing. To the left was the blacksmith's, pictured elsewhere, and to the right the barn used by Mr. Ward, the plumber. The corner has changed with the demolition of the large cottage in 1925.

155. Blacksmiths rest outside the smithy at the top of London Hill, *c*.1906.

156. London Hill, *c*.1902. This was once the main road from London to Rayleigh and beyond, but, due to its steepness at the top and the arrival of the railway, Crown Hill became favoured instead.

157. Crown Hill from the Mount, *c.*1900.

158.　A view from Downhall Road, *c*.1910.

159.　The moat at the Mount looked its best in 1920, but dried out in 1921 during the hot summer. The bridge, installed by E. B. Francis who owned the Mount at the time, no longer exists.

160.   View from the Mount showing the station and Devenish's buildings facing it.

161.   Dutch Cottage, Sweeps Row, Crown Hill and the pathway to Love Lane, in 1875.

162. Built by a breakaway faction of the Baptists in 1897-8, this Tabernacle became the Congregational church in 1910. This picture was taken from what was the Knoll, which has now been built on.

163. Caley Memorial Hall, seen here c.1920, was erected in memory of the Rev. A. Caley B.D., Rector of Rayleigh 1643-63. The attractive fence was replaced later by a brick wall.

164. Caley Memorial Hall: the account rendered by J. Byford, who built it.

165. Dutch Cottage on Crown Hill (viewed from the rear) was built in 1621 by refugees from Holland who were fleeing from persecution. Many settled on Canvey and helped to drain the island. When it was threatened with destruction, c.1900, Mr. R. E. Wakelin saved the cottage. Later it was purchased by public subscription, and through the generosity of Reg Byford and Victor Curtis, in 1950.

166.   The railway came in 1889 and was largely responsible for the rapid growth in the population. At one time Rayleigh had its own station master and several staff, as the goods depot and coalyard were hives of industry. Electricity and road transport changed that. The picture is of the station entrance, largely unchanged today.

167.   A steam engine awaiting its turn to use the single line to Southend. In the distance on the left is the old prison on Hangman's Field.

168. Rayleigh Gas Company opened in 1859. Gas was piped from the Southend works on the seafront. Later a large holder was erected near the station.

169. The old prison at Down Hall, c.1908, faced Hangman's Field and the corner was called Three Want Way until the railway came in 1889.

170. Down Hall, on the site of the ancient manor of the same name, has disappeared, as also has Harbegers which held lands towards Rawreth. In the 15th century, Down Hall belonged to Richard, Duke of York.

171. In 1926 eight or nine urns dating from the Iron Age were found buried on Hamborough Hill (Hambro Hill). Rochford Hundred is rich in such pottery and these are excellent examples.

172. Hambro Hill was a favoured area for settlers throughout the ages and several finds have been registered thereabouts. This photograph dates from *c.*1911 and shows the view from the Down Hall junction.

173.   Mr. W. Victor Curtis, O.B.E. was a distinguished personality who worked tirelessly for the people of Rayleigh. He was Chairman of the Rayleigh Urban District Council for a record four occasions. Here he is (right) with his sister, Miss K. Curtis, and the Clerk of the Council, Mr. C. E. FitzGerald, M.B.E., and his wife about to leave for a garden party at Buckingham Palace.

174.   The Rayleigh Council Chamber in 1960, showing the joint authors, Councillor Ernest H. Lane, J.P., in the Chair and, to his right, Edward FitzGerald, Clerk of the Council. The furniture, of high quality Honduras mahogany produced between 1870 and 1880, was purchased for £300, and its valuation today is many times in excess of that figure.

The Estate of J. DEVENISH, deceased, and ELIZA GROUT, deceased.

RAYLEIGH, ESSEX.

PARTICULARS AND CONDITIONS OF SALE

OF

THREE CAPITAL PLOTS

OF

Freehold Building Land

In CROWN LANE, RAYLEIGH

ALSO

THE VALUABLE ENCLOSURE OF

Freehold Pasture Land

KNOWN AS

Hambro Field, Rayleigh

Situated at the junction of Hambro Lane with the Main Road from Rayleigh to Hockley
and having extensive frontages both to the Main Road and Hambro Lane.

Let to Mr. William Finch at the very moderate rental of

PER £7 : 10 ANN.

Which will be offered for Sale by Auction, by

Messrs. Watson, Temple & Waymouth

At the "Golden Lion" Hotel, Rayleigh,

On SATURDAY, MAY 25TH, 1912.

At 4.30 o'clock in the Afternoon in Two Lots.

Copies of these Particulars may be had of—

The Solicitors:
Messrs. WOOD, SON & LANGTON,
Southend-on-Sea.

and of

THE AUCTIONEERS:
Southend and Westcliff-on-Sea.

Telephones—34 and 251, Southend.